Practicing What Jesus Preached

Practicing What Jesus Preached

A Month-Long Journey of Reflection,
Practice, and Prayer

Stephen Chapin Garner

Foreword by Joe Scarborough

CASCADE *Books* • Eugene, Oregon

PRACTICING WHAT JESUS PREACHED
A Month-Long Journey of Reflection, Practice, and Prayer

Cascade Books
An Imprint of Wipf and Stock Publishers
199 W. 8th Ave., Suite 3
Eugene, OR 97401

www.wipfandstock.com

PAPERBACK ISBN: 978-1-6667-6304-1
HARDCOVER ISBN: 978-1-6667-6305-8
EBOOK ISBN: 978-1-6667-6306-5

Cataloguing-in-Publication data:

Names: Garner, Stephen Chapin, author. | Scarborough, Joe, foreword.

Title: Practicing what Jesus preached : a month-long journey of reflection, practice, and prayer / Stephen Chapin Garner; foreword by Joe Scarborough.

Description: Eugene, OR: Cascade Books, 2023

Identifiers: ISBN 978-1-6667-6304-1 (paperback) | ISBN 978-1-6667-6305-8 (hardcover) | ISBN 978-1-6667-6306-5 (ebook)

Subjects: LCSH: Sermon on the Mount—Devotional use. | Christian life.

Classification: BT380 G26 2023 (print) | BT380 (ebook)

05/15/23

Tammie, Sam, Taylor, and Emma . . .
I thank God for you each and every day.

Contents

Foreword

When I was a younger man, I was a fretful flier. Dread would often overtake my emotions in the days leading up to my flight. A recurring fear would be that some ghastly fate would befall me at thirty thousand feet and leave my four children fatherless. I would occasionally scribble hurried notes before rushing to the airport. Though I can mercifully remember little of what I wrote then, I am sure I passed along the quote of some great statesman, a favorite Bible verse, and maybe a few lines from Hemingway's "A Moveable Feast."

As my children and I grew older, and I became more comfortable in my airplane seat, I gained a better perspective of exactly what quotes, verses, and passages my children and I needed to focus on to live a more fulfilled life. All these years later, my answer is now simple: read the Sermon on the Mount.

In three short chapters, Jesus reveals the essence of Christianity. He guides his followers to be merciful, to be peacemakers, to forgive each other, and to even love those who hate them. There is nothing here that remotely builds on the dogmatic framework of Christian nationalism, a prosperity gospel, or the slew of other heretical teachings that do grave damage to the church's mission. Perhaps that is why Chapin Garner's inspiring devotional on the Sermon on the Mount is more timely than ever. Chapin walks us through Christ's sermon with the kind of insight and wisdom that made him our family's most beloved pastor.

Foreword

There is no preacher I would rather learn from on any given Sunday than Chapin Garner, and with his work here focusing on the centerpiece of Christ's ministry on earth, this devotional will remain in our family for years to come. Perhaps one day, when a grandchild asks about the meaning of life, their mom or dad can reach up on the shelf and hand this devotional to them with the simple instruction, "Read this book."

Joe Scarborough

Acknowledgments

When it comes to matters of faith, no work of any weight or merit is an individual enterprise, and I am grateful that I have received such faithful assistance from so many dear friends. Having listened to years of sermons from our church balcony, his favorite perch, Joe Scarborough kindly agreed to provide the foreword. I'm thankful to former colleagues Debbie Chapman and Eric Dupee, who painstakingly edited this volume multiple times, and who offered helpful insight and suggestions for the daily practices, respectively. Our Men's Small Group Ministry and Collegiate Fellowship allowed me the opportunity to test this material in many of our conversations and gatherings. Even the front cover photo was a gift from a good friend—Dutch Doscher—who captured an illuminated moment on a Sunday morning during the pandemic, as I watched our congregation make their way up the hill in front of our church for worship. Most especially, I am so very grateful to God for my beloved Tammie and her tireless efforts to advise over the years on every sermon delivered and every book written. I could not be in ministry without her faithful support and partnership. The collaboration on this work reminds me yet again that, indeed, God is so very good, and family and friends are a blessing beyond compare!

Introduction

Why does the world need another book about Jesus? What difference will yet another series of reflections on the Sermon on the Mount make to anyone? The honest answer may be *"it is not needed, and it makes little difference."* However, as a person of faith, as a husband, a father, and a pastor, this is a volume I *need* in order to be a more committed and compassionate Christian.

For years I have had a nagging sense that the intimacy and immediacy of relationship with Jesus that I so long for can only come from trying to live as Jesus has commanded. This is a simple observation, but it has proved to be an elusive practice. This volume is an effort to find ways to meditate upon and practice living Jesus' desires for us, as outlined in his most famous sermon. We do have the ability to draw closer to our Lord and Savior when we are intentional about following Jesus' word, will, and way. Jesus' Sermon on the Mount might be viewed as his suggested constitution for the kingdom of God. If that is so, following the constitution might be the best way of knowing the King!

This devotional guide offers thirty-one reflections on Jesus' Sermon on the Mount. It offers a month-long opportunity to practice what Jesus preached and taught during his Galilean ministry. Each reflection is followed by a question for consideration, a practice to engage in, and a prayer for guidance and support. The emphasis of this exercise is practice, not perfection. Verse by verse, point by point, day by day, we attempt to implement Jesus' instruction. We will succeed at times, and falter at others, but with

Jesus' assistance and presence, our relationship with our Lord will continue to deepen. We will find that being Christian means a daily commitment and recommitment to practicing what Jesus preached.

One final note before the journey begins: Jesus' teaching does not make much sense apart from resurrection. As the apostle Paul testified to the Corinthians, "If for this life only we have hoped in Christ, we are of all people most to be pitied" (1 Cor 15:19). If we follow Jesus' commands with the belief that a materially better and more successful life will follow, we are likely to be disappointed. When we realize, however, that our life with Jesus extends into eternity, making sacrifices for faith and for others in this life becomes a more manageable and meaningful task. We live and serve to the glory of God and for the good of the world, trusting that any loss we experience in this life, is gain in the next. With a resurrection perspective, practicing what Jesus preached can be the thrill of a lifetime, and a crowning achievement that will last forever.

Come to Jesus

When Jesus saw the crowds, he went up the mountain;
and after he sat down, his disciples came to him.

MATTHEW 5:1

Reflection: A relationship with Jesus begins with a choice. Will you come to him? Do you desire a connection with the Lord? Do you long to be in the presence of the Christ? If so, you must choose to approach. The Gospels attest that scores of people made their way to Jesus. Some would be disciples, some were well-intentioned spiritual seekers, some were merely curious onlookers, and others would prove to be opponents. Whatever the intention or interest that motivates you, a relationship with Jesus begins with a desire to be with him, to make your way to him, to approach.

It is more than possible that the desire within us for union with Jesus is a mystical and internal response to his call on our lives. Our longing is evidence of his invitation to us. Whatever has drawn you to this classic mountaintop sermon, to read his words, and to pick up this book—trust your impulse. Draw closer. Read more carefully. Be intentional. A relationship with our living Lord begins by approaching him.

Practicing What Jesus Preached

Question: Are you ready to approach Jesus?

Practice: Set aside a specific time to come to Jesus using this guide for the next thirty-one days. Keep that time sacred and holy, and do not allow your approach to be interrupted. Imagine this time as your personal "appointment with Jesus." You might want to actually put "JC" in your calendar so you don't schedule over your time with the Lord!

Prayer: Lord, I long for you. I desire a deeper connection with you. I want a union with you that can bridge the divide and distance I often feel between us. Lord, I am aware that the connection and commitment I seek is likely inspired by you and your calling on my life. I will trust the impulse in my heart, and dare to approach you to the best of my ability. I pray that you assist me when I falter, and usher me into your presence. In your name, I pray. Amen.

Teachable

*Then he began to speak, and taught them . . . Now when Jesus had
finished saying these things, the crowds were astounded at his teaching,
for he taught them as one having authority, and not as their scribes.*

MATTHEW 5:2 & 7:28–29

Reflection: Of all the many titles and roles Jesus took on during his
earthly ministry, none was more important to him than the role of
rabbi—teacher. Jesus understood that his primary purpose was to
teach people how to live in right relationship with God and with
other people. Scripture attests that he did so with authority—like
the teachers we have found to be truly compelling in our lives. In
fact, when considering who Jesus was and how he taught, it might
be helpful to imagine Jesus having abilities similar to the instruc-
tors who have been most influential for us.

One of the first questions those of us who decide to be Christians need to ask and answer for ourselves is whether we want to
be a student. We need to be honest with ourselves. Am I willing to
learn? Will I take instruction? Am I open to having my mind and
my heart and my spirit challenged and changed? On our best days
we want our answer to be a resounding *"Yes!"* However, more often
than not, our actions, assumptions, and biases express a different

intention entirely. Many of us think we know best. We don't like to be told what to do, particularly if we don't like the command. We prefer to instruct others rather than take direction ourselves.

Again, to follow Jesus Christ the teacher, we need to be forthright with ourselves and with our Lord. Are we teachable? Are we coachable? Are we willing to learn, or relearn, how to live? If the answer is "Yes," then Jesus has all he needs to begin to work with us and on us. If the answer is something other than "Yes," we may not be ready for a deeper commitment with the Lord, or we might not allow Jesus the kind of access to us he desires. Being Christian means being honest with ourselves and the Lord. Being Christian means possessing a willingness to learn. Being Christian means following Jesus' instruction whether or not we understand it, believe it, or initially agree with it.

Question: Are you teachable?

Practice: In conjunction with this devotional guide, begin to keep a simple journal of your daily practices during these thirty-one days. What is your plan for practice as you begin your day? What were the challenges you encountered as you practiced throughout the day? What have you learned in your efforts to put Jesus' teaching into action? Make some brief notes at the beginning and the end of each day to track your progress.

Prayer: Lord, I dearly want to study with you. I want your words and your ways to redesign my life and my living. I want to be coachable and teachable and open to change. And yet, I know that I often inadvertently or deliberately resist instruction. I live so much of my life as if I know best, when deep down I know I have so very much to learn. Please cultivate within me an inquisitive mind, an open heart, and a receptive spirit. I desire to learn from your words and live in your ways. In your name, I pray. Amen.

Blessed

Blessed are the poor in spirit, for theirs is the kingdom of heaven.
Blessed are those who mourn, for they will be comforted.
Blessed are the meek, for they will inherit the earth.

MATTHEW 5:3-5

Reflection: As the crowds gathered around him, Jesus sat down and he began his most famous sermon by making nine statements about "blessing." Jesus proclaimed that the poor in spirit, the mournful, the meek, the hungry, and many others who were often overlooked, were "blessed." This was a radical proposition, and would have likely been quite surprising to Jesus' first-century Jewish audience. It was a prevailing belief at the time that physical, material, and relational well-being were associated with God's blessing and favor. Someone who was rich, healthy, and surrounded by numerous children, was understood to be blessed and favored by God. Good fortune was believed to be evidence of God's satisfaction with an individual, and with communities as a whole. Conversely, if a person was ill, poor, or childless, their low estate and misfortune were attributed to being under the curse of God. It seemed to make sense, and perhaps makes sense to us, or at least it aligns with our understanding of fairness: good people should receive good things, and bad people should reap what they sow.

It might be helpful, however, to our contemporary ears and minds to interpret the word "blessed" as "beloved." Throughout the Bible, Scripture asserts that God pays special attention to, and takes particular interest in, people the world often overlooks. Poor folks, grieving people, hungry individuals, hold a special place in God's heart. Whether or not they feel or appear to be blessed, they are dearly beloved. When we find ourselves down and out, disheartened, or discounted we too must remember our belovedness.

What would it mean for us and for the world if we took special interest in people who live on the margins of our lives and our communities? What would it mean if we took as much interest in those who are overlooked and underappreciated as Jesus did? How might inequity and neglect be mitigated if we paid attention to the introduction of Jesus' most memorable sermon? Jesus began his Sermon on the Mount affirming a truth he understood and wanted each of us to learn: God dearly loves those our world often overlooks.

Question: What does it mean to you to be beloved and blessed?

Practice: Reach out to someone you know who is overlooked or underappreciated and tell them something you value about them. Bless them.

Prayer: Lord God, you value the lost, the least, and the lonely. You care deeply for those people I often overlook or choose to ignore. Any and every message from you begins with a call to compassion and care for those who are disrespected and discounted. Everyone is of value and of importance to you, Lord God. Whether I am feeling particularly blessed, or feel as if I am under a curse . . . help me to understand your deep love for me, and help me to share that love and blessing with others. In Jesus' name, I pray. Amen.

God's Values

Blessed are those who hunger and thirst for righteousness, for they will be filled. Blessed are the merciful, for they will receive mercy. Blessed are the pure in heart, for they will see God. Blessed are the peacemakers, for they will be called children of God.

MATTHEW 5:6-9

Reflection: Having established God's interest and affection for people that are often regarded as less important and least valued in our world, Jesus spoke about another group of people whom God favors. Those who do the work of faith and who live by the virtues of God are dearly beloved and richly blessed. God prizes people who desire to live rightly: who are merciful, who are pure in heart, and who work for peace.

To hunger and thirst for righteousness does not mean that someone has perfectly aligned their life with the will of God—but the *desire* to do what is right is pleasing to the Lord. The willingness to be merciful—to give to others better than one receives—is a godly characteristic that is delightful to the Lord. To be pure in heart—to have your internal interests and intentions correctly and thoughtfully focused—pleases God to no end. When you assist people to cooperate instead of fight, when you help to draw people together instead of separate, when you work for unity and heal division, you mend the human family as God intended.

Whereas the first three Beatitudes are conditions anyone might find themselves in, the next four Beatitudes focus on commitments anyone can choose to make and keep. They are all characteristics that God employs when engaging humanity, and when we choose to intentionally work with others as God has chosen to abide with us, the blessings and promises offered are both expansive and divine. We are made whole. We receive the kindness we offer. We see the Spirit of God alive and active in the world. We prove by our actions to be the Lord's family here on earth.

Question: Which virtue would be the easiest for you to practice, and which is most challenging—righteousness, mercy, purity of heart, peacemaking? Why?

Practice: On a note card, write down the names of people you know who epitomizes each of these virtues. Keep those names where you can see them throughout the day. Consider how you might live more like they live.

Prayer: Lord, I desire to live rightly, to be kind to others, to be pure of mind and heart, and to live peaceably with those around me. I long to live by the virtues you promise to use in your relationship with me. However, my efforts are often faltering and too easily surrendered. I pray that the hunger and thirst to live in ways that are pleasing to you is a worthy place to start. Help me to grow in faith from someone with good intentions, to someone who engages in right actions. In Jesus' name, I pray. Amen.

Persecution

Blessed are those who are persecuted for righteousness' sake, for theirs is the kingdom of heaven. Blessed are you when people revile you and persecute you and utter all kinds of evil against you falsely on my account. Rejoice and be glad, for your reward is great in heaven, for in the same way they persecuted the prophets who were before you.

MATTHEW 5:10-12

Reflection: There is no guarantee that doing the right thing or fighting for a just cause will win one praise or affirmation. We live in a world where you are often "damned if you do, and damned if you don't," "where no good deed goes unpunished," and nice guys and girls are said to "finish last." Advocating for that which needs to change, confronting abuse and injustice, and speaking truth, even in love, can get a person into a heap of trouble. While there are certainly times when truth and goodwill win out, when a person challenges a system that has been in place for a long time, or confronts a situation that is harmful but accepted as normal, or objects to a process that keeps the peace at the cost of the dignity of others, the prospect of change can produce blowback. Even the most well-intentioned and careful "prophets" can find themselves in the crosshairs of others, facing persecution.

It was a well-known reality in ancient Israel that the prophets of God, advocating for change, were often the object of persecution. Jesus himself referred to Jerusalem as "the city that kills the prophets" (Matthew 23:37). We have plenty of contemporary examples of prophets—truthtellers advocating for a more just and equitable world—who have been maligned, persecuted, and have even lost their lives. If someone is called by God to speak truth in a world where convenient lies and unjust practices frame daily life, the cost can be painfully high. As followers of Jesus, we should know that the cost of doing good in the world can be the cross.

However, while persecution may be the worldly reward for trying to speak and act and think rightly, Jesus said that the eternal reward for living and advocating for life as God wants it to be lived, is great. Jesus was clear: those who choose to spend and expend their lives working for peace, justice, and dignity for all, will be inheritors of the kingdom of heaven and God's blessing. They will take their place in a long and distinguished line of faithful prophets who experienced persecution in life and eternal glory beyond death.

Question: What is something you know needs to be done or changed for good?

Practice: Think of an issue in your community that you perceive as unjust or unfair. Begin to draft a letter to the editor of your local news outlet. What should you say? What tone should the letter take? Write it. Pray about what you have written, and by the end of the week decide if you will send it in.

Prayer: Lord, I do not want to walk out into a world looking for abuses or injustices to address. Championing truth and righteousness are not primary causes in my life. I am not looking for a fight, even if one needs to be had for the welfare of others and the good of the world. My reluctance is fueled, in part, by my ignorance of what is good, right, and just. It can be wildly presumptuous and annoyingly self-righteous to assume I can be an arbiter of that which is right. But I know when something is wrong, and I suspect my reluctance to speak has something to do with a lack of courage, a faltering of will, and a hesitation to upset the status quo. Help me to know when to speak up and when to be silent, when to step forward and when to step back, when to remain in place and when to be prophetic. In your name, I pray. Amen.

DAY 6

Salt of the Earth

You are the salt of the earth; but if salt has lost its taste,
how can its saltiness be restored? It is no longer good for
anything, but is thrown out and trampled under foot.

MATTHEW 5:13

Reflection: Jesus looked out at a swelling crowd on a hillside on the western bank of the Sea of Galilee. People came from the towns around the lake, but others traveled from long distances—the cities of the Decapolis, Judea, Syria, and beyond. The crowd was made up of fishermen, tradespeople, the unemployed, the desperately needy, and those who were breaking under the oppression of the Roman Empire. Jesus looked out at these poor, dear people and told them: You *are* the salt of the earth. Not you *can be*, or you *should be* salt of the earth—you *are* the salt of the earth.

Salt was a very valuable mineral in antiquity. Salt was used to enhance the flavor of meals, but more importantly, it was a primary preservative for food, and it was used for healing because of its antibacterial and antiseptic properties. Salt was also added to temple offerings to make them holy and acceptable to God. For Jesus to tell the marginalized people who made their way to him that they were salt was significant and unexpected praise. Jesus was saying that these dear folks were of incredible value—they were a source of healing, preserving, and healing holiness among God's people, with an ability to spice things up as needed. While the crowds who followed Jesus were hoping and praying and longing for life to change for the better, Jesus didn't want them to lose the characteristics that made them special and beloved by God—they were to strive to retain their saltiness.

In our lexicon today, "the salt of the earth" is an expression for a very good and honest person—or group of people—folks who embody the best and noblest elements of society. As Jesus looked at the people who had traveled from far and near to listen to him, he saw in them something they may not have seen in themselves: goodness, faithfulness, value. Jesus saw people who had within them the power to heal a broken world, to preserve the values of the Lord, who made the earth holy and beloved by their mere presence in it.

Question: As an aspiring follower of Jesus yourself, how does it feel for Jesus to say *you are* a healing agent, one who preserves traditions and values, an individual whose presence in the world makes God's creation holy?

Practice: Identify someone who is ailing in body, mind, or spirit— call them to touch base, prepare them a meal to cheer their spirits, send them flowers, or arrange to make a visit to see them sometime this week. Bring healing and happiness to someone who is struggling.

Prayer: Lord, I am reluctant to think of myself as one who brings wholeness, preservation, and holiness into your world. I am more acquainted with my glaring defects than my beneficial qualities. But you have said that your people are healing, preserving, and sanctifying ingredients in the world. Help me to live out the best and most noble of human characteristics as I make my way through the day. In your name, I pray. Amen.

Light of the World

You are the light of the world. A city built on a hill cannot be hid. No one after lighting a lamp puts it under the bushel basket, but on the lampstand, and it gives light to all in the house. In the same way, let your light shine before others, so that they may see your good works and give glory to your Father in heaven.

MATTHEW 5:14–16

Reflection: As Jesus preached on the hillside in Galilee, he noted his surroundings and wove them into his message as sermon illustrations. Just to the south of where Jesus sat and taught was the recently established city of Tiberius. Tiberius was being constructed by King Herod Antipas to honor the second emperor of Rome, Tiberius Caesar. The city was built from the shoreline of the Sea of Galilee up a steep slope to the east. At night, Tiberius's lights would have stretched from the water's edge up to the crown of the mount it was built upon. The construction and the growing illumination of Tiberius would have been one of the most notable events in the region.

When Jesus told his followers that "you are the light of the world" and your light shouldn't be hidden any more than a city on a hill can be obscured, he was likely referencing how the city of Tiberius was visible for miles because of its nighttime illumination.

What Jesus is indicating is that just like an illuminated city on a hill, our lives and our living can brighten the world. Much like the characteristics of light itself, our lives can provide clarity, illumination, and even a degree of warmth in an often dark and cold world. Our living—our shining forth—can be so radiant that life gets more navigable, not just for ourselves and those closest to us, but even for those at great distances. Jesus said "you *are* light"—shine, radiate God's goodness into the world!

The outcome and purpose of our illuminating presence, as Jesus described it, would have been a noticeable contrast to that of the city of Tiberius. Tiberius was being built to honor Caesar. The city was established to curry favor with Rome. Tiberius's light was to shine forth as a tribute to the empire and to remind all who saw it what authority was ultimately in control. Jesus said that our light shines forth not for our own glory, not for the recognition of any earthly monarch, but so that God's good works might be seen and made known in the world. Tiberius was built for the emperor's glory, you were made for God's glory!

Question: What prevents you from letting your light shine for others to see?

Practice: When you have the opportunity to perform a good work or task today—especially if that work is laborious or ill-timed— imagine doing the work for the glory of God. Your good effort at an inconvenient but necessary time shines forth God's goodness in the world.

Prayer: Lord, it is difficult to think of myself as light. I feel like I live in the darkness of confusion and uncertainty so much of the time. Help me to believe what you claim about me—that my life and my living are part of your plan to illuminate the world. Help your light to shine through me as a beacon to those around me. Not my light, but your light. Shine through me today. In Jesus' name, I pray. Amen.

DAY 8

Law Abiding

*Do not think that I have come to abolish the law or the prophets;
I have come not to abolish but to fulfill. For truly I tell you, until
heaven and earth pass away, not one letter, not one stroke of a
letter, will pass from the law until all is accomplished.*

MATTHEW 5:17-18

Reflection: Jesus was considered by the religious leaders of his day
to be a lawbreaker—or, at the very least, a teacher who was fairly
dismissive of the Hebrew legal code. Jesus argued with and challenged local scribes and Pharisees who were attempting to ensure
the purity and holiness of the Jewish people. Jesus was seemingly
cavalier in his observance of Sabbath—he performed healing
miracles, and even had his students gather food on the Hebrew
day of rest. When he arrived in the temple—the center of Jewish
faith observance—Jesus took issue with temple administration
and practice. He flew into a rage and began turning over tables of
money changers and driving out anyone who was buying or selling
in and around God's house. To religious leaders who took seriously the maintaining of the letter of God's law, Jesus appeared to
present a concerning challenge to faithful observance.

Likewise, as Christians, we can often assume Jesus was something other than he was. We might look at Jesus and think he was the very first Christian. We might come to believe that Jesus was the leader of a new and improved form of faith. Or, we believe that Jesus was remarkably original in his thinking, teaching, and living. The religious leaders of Jesus' day, and many of us today, often miss the fact that Jesus was not particularly original, nor was he trying to create some new kind of faith. Jesus was Jewish and he desired to draw people into a deeper connection with God. So many of Jesus' teachings and prayers—those we may think of as unique or a departure from traditional Hebrew understanding—are either a restatement or rearticulation of ancient Jewish Scripture and law. For instance, many Christians believe that Jesus' reduction of Hebrew law into two basic commands—love God and love neighbor—was wildly inventive. In fact, Jesus was just repeating two brief sections of the law that are found in the books of Deuteronomy and Leviticus.

Jesus was a deeply committed Jew. Jesus knew Scripture. Jesus loved God. Jesus understood Hebrew law and was committed to helping people just like us fulfill it. Jesus did not come into the world to abolish that which was old and establish something new. Jesus came preaching and teaching in ways that breathed new life and understanding into a rich, ancient, and holy faith tradition. Jesus was not a lawbreaker, but an interpreter of faith intent to help us learn, grow, and obey.

Question: Why did the religious leaders of his day misunderstand Jesus, and why do we?

Practice: One day this week commit to obeying the commandment to "Remember the Sabbath and keep it holy." Rest for an entire day. Refrain from labor. Delight in the goodness of creation, and give thanks to God for it.

Prayer: Lord, I often think of you as blazing a new trail and advocating for an improved way of being faithful. You encourage all people toward renewed faithfulness, but you do so grounded in the faith promises and faith history that were established at the foundation of the earth. You followed the commands of faith unwaveringly, and the gates of paradise were opened to you. Help me to take the laws and commands of faith seriously, so that the rule God established for me to live by might be a blessing to me now, and on into eternity. In your name, I hope and pray. Amen.

Realm of God

*Therefore, whoever breaks one of the least of these commandments,
and teaches others to do the same, will be called least in the kingdom of
heaven; but whoever does them and teaches them will be called great in the
kingdom of heaven. For I tell you, unless your righteousness exceeds that
of the scribes and Pharisees, you will never enter the kingdom of heaven.*

MATTHEW 5:19-20

Reflection: After addressing one of the charges leveled against
him—that he was a lawbreaker—Jesus turned on the scribes and
Pharisees to insist that adherence to laws great and small was essential to one's entrance and position in heaven. Apparently, religious teaching of Jesus' day had a hierarchy—some commands
were viewed as essential to uphold, such as Sabbath restrictions,
whereas other rules could be amended or overlooked. One of the
classic examples that Jesus addressed was the temple and syna-
gogue practice of allowing Jews to forego their responsibility to
provide for their parents in their old age, as long as they made
a generous financial contribution to the religious establishment.
In the teaching that follows, Jesus' instruction is actually far more
rigorous than Levitical law. Jesus' expectation was that following
the precepts of God is essential to a life that is pleasing to the Lord.

In fact, Jesus indicates in this passage that the legalism engaged in by scribes and Pharisees served to bind people, whereas Jesus' understanding of the spirit and purpose of God's law was to free people for loving existence with God and one another.

Jesus' assertion in this passage is that the adherence to, and teaching of, God's law allows access to the realm of God. In Jesus' continual effort to help connect people with God, Jesus knew that fidelity to the instructions of God was a way to deeper union with the Lord—in this life and in the next. To live by God's commands, to allow the laws of God to inform and form one's life, to live trusting that God's rules are set in place for our well-being and flourishing, allows for a dynamic, meaningful, and impactful existence. For people who dare to live by the designs and desires of God—who choose to intentionally follow the leading of the Lord—there is an awesome discovery and realization that the ways of God really work. God's outline for life is not restrictive, but life-affirming and life-giving. To choose to practice the precepts of faith, and to teach others to do the same, is so much more rewarding and freeing than trying to figure everything out by one's self.

As Jesus began to transition his sermon into a series of commands of his own, he wanted his listeners to understand that a life lived in fidelity to God's will and desires brings us closer to the Lord. Fulfilling commands set in place for our own good and the good of the world brings us into closer union with God. The kingdom of heaven—the very realm of God—is accessed through obedience.

Question: Why do you think obedience to God can be so difficult?

Practice: Make two lists. What do you want? What does God ask of you? Compare and contrast those two lists.

Prayer: Lord, I too often chafe at commands. I don't like to be told what to do and what not to do. I like to be free to do as I please. And yet, Lord, my own choices haven't always met with the results I have desired. My relationships are more challenging than I like to admit, my work feels laborious and lacks meaning, and my sense of purpose and enthusiasm for life and the activities I engage in are dampened.

Realm of God

I want to be invigorated, I want to live in essential ways, I want to feel close to you. As I delve more deeply into Jesus' sermon, and the directions and decisions he will encourage me to make, build in me a resolve to try to practice what he preached, so I might live as he lived, and lives . . . living well now, and dwelling in your eternal presence forever. In Jesus' name, I pray. Amen.

Raising the Bar

You have heard that it was said to those of ancient times, "You shall not murder"; and "whoever murders shall be liable to judgment." But I say to you that if you are angry with a brother or sister, you will be liable to judgment; and if you insult a brother or sister, you will be liable to the council; and if you say, "You fool," you will be liable to the hell of fire.

MATTHEW 5:21-22

Reflection: Having addressed the concerns of religious leaders who were listening to him, Jesus began to articulate his own under-standing of the law, and the spirit which undergirded the com-mands of God. Jesus' instructions to his followers clearly raised the bar on what thoughtful and faithful living entailed. Jesus was aware that killing and violence take many forms. While there was a well-defined prohibition against taking life, there were other forms of assault that were truly harmful in Jesus' understanding. It is not acceptable to kill someone, nor is it acceptable to assassinate some-one's character. It is wrong to physically harm someone, and it is also wrong to damage someone emotionally or psychologically. It is not only against God's will to tear someone limb from limb, it is also against God's desires to tear someone asunder with harmful words spoken to their face or behind their back. For Jesus, violence is violence, no matter the form it takes. Physical, emotional, and verbal abuse are all reprehensible to God.

This understanding of faithful living was much more expansive than Jewish law of Jesus' day required. Jesus was aware that doing harm to another went well beyond what can be physically seen and felt. Hurt comes in many forms, and people committed to love, kindness, and peace need to understand and adhere to practices of living that build up instead of break down. For anyone who thought Jesus might be willing to bend or break rules and regulations, his own commands reflect how high his expectations were for his followers. The crime to be avoided in this passage isn't just murder, it is the anger and rage that can lead to any kind of assault. To follow Jesus means to live with very high expectations. Jesus truly raised the bar on religious rules!

Question: How can your thoughts be as destructive or as egregious as your actions?

Practice: Consider someone you often complain about. Find an occasion to offer praise for that person in the company of others and in their hearing.

Prayer: Lord, I may not do physical harm to anyone, but my words, my anger, and my aggressive tendencies can be punishing in their own way. Sticks and stones do damage, but words hurt too . . . and sometimes emotional pain lasts longer than that which afflicts the body. Help me to ease up when I feel angry. Help me to hold my tongue when I am tempted to offer biting critique. Help me to be generous when I begin to get aggressive or hostile. Help me to be more like you. In your name, I pray. Amen.

Pleasing Offering

So when you are offering your gift at the altar, if you remember that your brother or sister has something against you, leave your gift there before the altar and go; first be reconciled to your brother or sister, and then come and offer your gift. Come to terms quickly with your accuser while you are on the way to court with him, or your accuser may hand you over to the judge, and the judge to the guard, and you will be thrown into prison. Truly I tell you, you will never get out until you have paid the last penny.

MATTHEW 5:23-26

Reflection: Jesus quickly shifted the focus of his message to reconciliation between people. More important than making an offering to God is making amends with people we have injured or offended in some way. We should not attempt to present ourselves to the Lord until we have set things right with the people with whom we are at odds. This aligns well with the Christian understanding that to love God means to live charitably and graciously with others. The best way to express love and devotion to the Lord is by living well and generously with those around us. For Jesus, loving God and loving neighbor were inseparable commands—you cannot have one without the other.

Pleasing Offering

One of the interesting features of the two expressions of reconciliation is that both examples assume those responsible for the relational challenge are Jesus' listeners—and by extension us! The assumption in the text is that someone may have "something against us" or that we have an "accuser" that might take us to court. It is a subtle but important inference. Jesus assumes that we bear some responsibility for any relational break, and therefore, we are to take the initiative to make amends and bring about reconciliation. The assumption of guilt on our part for relational rifts is unlikely to sit well with us. However, when a relationship breaks down, there tends to be more than enough blame to go around. While "guilt" for a broken relationship may lie more with one person than another, we all bear a degree of responsibility when relationships are damaged.

As Christians, in a faith tradition that emphasizes the need for forgiveness to sustain relationships, Jesus charges us to be the ones to make the first move towards reconciliation. God doesn't care about any offering more than our gift of forgiveness toward others. Jesus wants us to be the ones to initiate efforts that mend rifts between people. Leave the altar to address relational issues. Come to terms with those with whom we are at odds. While the work of reconciliation may be difficult and even unpalatable to us, the rationale is clear. If God has forgiven us so that we are reconciled to God, we must make the same offerings to others. In fact, reconciliation is the best gift one could ever offer the Lord!

Question: Who is someone with whom you are currently at odds?

Practice: Reach out to someone with whom you are currently at odds: a friend, a family member, a co-worker, a neighbor. Thoughtfully acknowledge the rift, and state how you believe you bear some of the responsibility for the break, and then work to resolution, or at least, a charitable peace.

Prayer: Lord, when I am at odds with someone, I tend to be more focused on how I have been offended than how I might have given offense. In fact, the thought of making an effort at reconciliation with someone I don't particularly care for is unpleasant to me. I'd rather discard certain relationships than work to reconcile them. And yet, I would not want that to be the way you deal with me when I offend you. I would not want you to discard me or discount the possibility of reestablishing relationship. When I pray the prayer you taught your people to offer, I speak the words "forgive my sins, as I forgive those who sin against me." In that prayer I ask you to be as forgiving of me as I am of others. Help me to be more forgiving and reconciling, so that I can continue to expect the same from you. In your name, I pray. Amen.

Radical Surgery

You have heard that it was said, "You shall not commit adultery." But
I say to you that everyone who looks at a woman with lust has already
committed adultery with her in his heart. If your right eye causes you to
sin, tear it out and throw it away; it is better for you to lose one of your
members than for your whole body to be thrown into hell. And if your right
hand causes you to sin, cut it off and throw it away; it is better for you
to lose one of your members than for your whole body to go into hell.

MATTHEW 5:27-30

Reflection: In the Gospel of Matthew, Jesus gets serious when it
comes to battling sin. If your eye causes you to sin, tear it out. If
your right hand causes you to sin, cut it off. Jesus is clearly being
hyperbolic, but when it comes to gaining victory over sin, Jesus
advocates decisive action. Tapering off, weaning off, cutting back
a bit on sinful behavior is not a significant enough adjustment.
When doing battle with sin, you have got to cut it out. Sin has a
cancerous quality to it; if we do not get serious about removing
the infirmity, it has a way of growing out of control and taking
over. Unchecked sin can lead to a kind of spiritual death, so Jesus
advocates radical action.

While we certainly need to pray for the Lord's assistance to address our sinful behavior—it is very difficult to perform surgery on one's self—there are steps we can take to address our unhealthy tendencies. If you are in the habit of whiling away the hours viewing pornography on the internet or gambling online, it's time to sever your connection. If you are engaging in an extramarital flirtation that threatens to turn into something more, it's time to delete the contact and stay out of touch. If you drink too much and get crude and hurtful when you are out with the guys or girls, it's time to hang out with different friends. If you are prone to negativity, gossip, and harsh critique of others, close your mouth—commit to a discipline of silence when you feel yourself tempted to speak ill of others. If you don't, Jesus is clear—you may find yourself in hell. When you are bound by sin, when you are being overrun by your lusts and swept away by your desires, it's time to get serious, it's time to cut it out, it's time for radical surgery. This is a hard, but important, word for those of us who desire to claim the freedom of forgiveness, love, and new life Jesus offers us.

Question: How would you define sin, and is there a particular sin you struggle with?

Practice: Make a choice to stop an unhealthy behavior today. Get rid of, or remove yourself from, whatever temptations are close at hand or within view. Pray for divine encouragement, and resolve to cut it out once and for all. Then, tell a trusted friend about your commitment, and ask them to keep you accountable as you address the specific temptation.

Prayer: Lord, you know where I falter. You know there are behaviors and vices that I need to remove from my life. You know how I desire to be a better person than I am. You also know, as well as I do, that I cannot do this on my own. I need you to help me break free from the sin that clings too closely to me. Please grant me the courage, strength, and resolve to cut sins from my life that keep me from you, and keep me from being the best me. In your name, I pray. Amen.

Divorced

*It was also said, "Whoever divorces his wife, let him give her a
certificate of divorce." But I say to you that anyone who divorces his
wife, except on the ground of unchastity, causes her to commit adultery;
and whoever marries a divorced woman commits adultery.*

MATTHEW 5:31–32

Reflection: If we find ourselves nodding our heads in agreement
with Jesus' teaching to this point, our comfort with Jesus' commands tends to shift as he addresses divorce. These two verses
seem both uncompromising and uncharitable. Most of us know
and love people who have been, or are, divorced. Family members
and friends—and perhaps even ourselves—have had to endure
relational breaks. This passage of Scripture can seem overly judg-
mental and callous, and we are tempted to dismiss this admonition
as not in keeping with the times, nor in line with our understanding of the grace that is needed to make sense of our personal histories and relational challenges.

However, people who immediately recoil from this particular teaching often miss out on the depth of what Jesus is trying
to communicate. While Jesus is certainly not in favor of divorce,
he is communicating something much more significant than mere

relational expectations. Taken with the teaching that immediately follows these two verses, you can begin to get a sense of Jesus' overarching concern—vows and commitments to others are serious matters. Vows should not be made or broken lightly. The promises we make should be kept as a sacred bond. Because of Jesus' assertion that a divorce is an acceptable response to adultery, we know that Jesus understood that there are certain behaviors or infidelities that would necessitate a relational break. Jesus does not affirm abuse. Jesus does not endorse neglect. Jesus does not encourage carelessness between people committed to one another. However, Jesus clearly believed that vows are serious business, and relationships should not be easily or cavalierly discarded.

There is one other truly important feature of this teaching of which we must not overlook: Jesus is also advocating for the protection of women. This is an important and prophetic theme in Jesus' ministry. In an age when women were considered property, a divorce could force a woman into poverty and even toward death. There were very few avenues of support for women who were given a certificate of divorce. Jesus understood that women were to be valued and treasured. Dismissing a wife because she displeased her husband was akin to breaking the sacred commandments of God. Jesus' prohibition of divorce was a form of advocacy for the care and welfare of women. Vows are to be honored, and wives are to be cherished. Do not take vows lightly, and take good care of those pledged to you. Care between people, and protection of the vulnerable are at the heart of Jesus' teaching on divorce.

Question: What is a vow or promise you have made that you need to recommit to?

Practice: Consider some of the vows you have taken throughout your life: baptismal, marital, or vocational. Look up the specific vows you would have committed to. Print them out and place them in this book for continual reference.

Prayer: Lord, I have made vows and broken them. I have made promises and backed out of them. I have given my word and not followed through on my commitment. Lord, I desire to be more faithful in my commitments. I am truly sorry for my failings, and I humbly repent. Forgive me. Absolve me. Allow me to begin again . . . to try again. And allow me to afford that same grace to those who are in relationship with me. In your name, I pray. Amen.

DAY 14

Speaking Plainly

Again, you have heard that it was said to those of ancient times, "You shall not swear falsely, but carry out the vows you have made to the Lord." But I say to you, Do not swear at all, either by heaven, for it is the throne of God, or by the earth, for it is his footstool, or by Jerusalem, for it is the city of the great King. And do not swear by your head, for you cannot make one hair white or black. Let your word be "Yes, Yes" or "No, No"; anything more than this comes from the evil one.

MATTHEW 5:33–37

Reflection: For anyone who is uncomfortable with Jesus' teaching of divorce in the preceding verses, his next few statements further clarify his primary intent: Jesus wants us to recognize that the making and taking of vows is very serious business. Jesus wasn't focused on chastising people who were enduring relational fractures, but rather, he was intent on impressing on his listeners—and us—the significance of vows made and taken. Pledging ourselves to others, making well-intentioned promises, committing or recommitting ourselves to God, is terribly important business. In fact, covenantal statements are such weighty matters, and our inability to keep our word is so commonplace, that Jesus suggests that it is better for us to refrain from swearing an oath about what we will or will not do. It is better to forego making a promise than to break our word!

Jesus' encouragement is that we get in the habit of speaking simply and plainly in all circumstances. Jesus said we should respond to requests made of us by saying *"yes"* or *"no";* any further commitment can be hazardous. In truth, too often we waffle and waver when something is asked of us. We say *"maybe,"* or *"I need to think about it,"* or *"I will try,"* when we know our answer should be a firm *"no."* We hem and haw, we make excuses and set conditions, we put off making decisions, even when we know our response should be a resounding *"yes."* Whether it's not wanting to disappoint people, or conversely, wanting to impress others with our emphatic commitment . . . both equivocating and overpromising are less than faithful and forthright ways to communicate and live.

Jesus wants people of faith like us to speak clearly and to act decisively—making grand promises, or vowing to do big things, or unwisely committing ourselves to more than we can accomplish is unwise and unfaithful. A simple "yes" or an honest "no" is often the best way to communicate our position on matters great and small. Speak plainly and clearly without making promises you can't keep. Do not give your word unless you are absolutely sure you can make good on it. If you do make vows and commitments, carry them out to their completion. We have all broken promises at times and failed to follow through on commitments we have made. Thankfully, Scripture asserts that God forgives us for those shortcomings. However, the goal is still before us—to be people of our word.

Question: What role does decisiveness play in following Jesus?

Practice: Make a list of things you should say "yes" to, and things to which you should say "no." Adhere to your list today.

Prayer: Lord, I too often make casual promises and give my word without fully counting the cost. There are too many times when I equivocate instead of speaking simply, clearly, and honestly. Help me to be more careful when I give my word, and give me resolve to make good on the commitments and vows I do make. Prompt in me a willingness to communicate clearly by offering a simple "yes" to that which I should do, or "no," rather than committing more than I can deliver. In Jesus' name, I pray. Amen.

Doing the Unexpected and Impossible

You have heard that it was said, "An eye for an eye and a tooth for a tooth." But I say to you, Do not resist an evildoer. But if anyone strikes you on the right cheek, turn the other also; and if anyone wants to sue you and take your coat, give your cloak as well; and if anyone forces you to go one mile, go also the second mile. Give to everyone who begs from you, and do not refuse anyone who wants to borrow from you.

MATTHEW 5:38-42

Reflection: At the end of the first chapter of Jesus' Sermon on the Mount, Jesus seems to be asking the impossible. Even if we love the Lord, and desire to both follow him and please him, this section of Matthew is where we often begin to lose a little heart and hope. Jesus raises the bar of faithful living to a level that can seem not only unmanageable, but ridiculously unwise. Do not put up a fight against people with ill intent? Turn the other cheek? When someone harms us or tries to harm us, we are to offer ourselves up for more punishment? This is like the lie we told ourselves when we were young, that it takes real courage to walk away from a fight. But we know better. Strong people don't let themselves get pushed around. Successful people stand their ground. Proud people don't back down from an altercation. The idea that when struck we would just take it, is simply not the way to succeed in life. If we give to everyone who begs from us we won't have anything left, and those doing the asking won't ever learn to fend for themselves— they will be perpetually dependent. If someone forces us to go one mile, that means they are stronger than we are, or have a degree of authority over us. The only way to regain our power is to refuse to bend to the demands of those who push us. Or, at least that is what we have come to believe!

What Jesus knew and taught is that for relationships to change, for intractable situations to be resolved, for the cycle of anger, resentment, and violence to abate in our lives and our world, we have to be willing to do the unexpected—perhaps even that which we deem impossible or imprudent. Meeting anger with love, meeting disappointment with hope, meeting judgment with mercy, holding back when we want to lash out, going the distance when we would rather give up—Jesus teaches us that is how people change and the world is transformed for good.

For if we recognize that our relational intuition and inclinations do not seem to be working particularly well, if choosing to navigate life by our own code of conduct instead of Jesus' instructions is not producing healthy, faithful, loving outcomes . . . should that not give us pause to consider a different path? If what we are doing is not working, might it not make sense to finally try to follow Jesus' relational instructions? Might it not be time to do the unexpected in the hope of changed and enhanced outcomes? What if "doing the impossible," or at least attempting it, is our best way to the relational transformation we desire?

Question: Think of a relationship, or a situation that involves others that is not going particularly well at the moment. How are your reactions, behaviors, or approach to the situation contributing to the difficult dynamic?

Practice: When you find yourself agitated with someone or something today, instead of reacting and responding with anger, resentment, or frustration, pause, breath, pray. And then attempt to respond with reserve, generosity, and patient endurance.

Prayer: Lord, I react so instinctively sometimes. I respond without thinking. I make gut decisions. I am more than willing to fight when challenged. I am part of a cycle of violence and careless living that keeps relationships in peril and your world in bondage. Somehow, I need to live differently, act differently, and respond differently if that cycle is ever to be broken. Help me to do the unexpected—that which I believe impossible—so that unhealthy patterns of living might change, in the world and also within me. In Jesus' name, I pray. Amen.

That All May Grow

You have heard that it was said, "You shall love your neighbor and hate your enemy." But I say to you, Love your enemies and pray for those who persecute you, so that you may be children of your Father in heaven; for he makes his sun rise on the evil and on the good, and sends rain on the righteous and on the unrighteous. For if you love those who love you, what reward do you have? Do not even the tax collectors do the same? And if you greet only your brothers and sisters, what more are you doing than others? Do not even the Gentiles do the same? Be perfect, therefore, as your heavenly Father is perfect.

MATTHEW 5:43-48

Reflection: Linked closely to the previous section of Jesus' sermon, Jesus' relational encouragement seems even more extreme. Love enemies. Pray for abusers. Be perfect as God is perfect. What could be more absurd! And yet, tucked in this little passage of Scripture is a kernel of divine wisdom that shouldn't be overlooked. There is good news for each and every one of us who is not yet living as the Lord desires for us to live.

We make judgments and evaluate people every day; in fact, we do this every moment of our lives. We judge and evaluate the situations we find ourselves in, as well as the opportunities and challenges we encounter. We try to figure out where our time and effort is best placed. We choose to invest ourselves in the good and promising employee. We focus our attention on the attractive and captivating man or woman. We even offer a bit more of ourselves to the child who is better behaved. We judge the good and the bad, and we invest ourselves accordingly.

Jesus tells us that this is not the way of God. God allows sun and rain to nourish the good and the evil, the just and the unjust, the righteous and the unrighteous. Sunlight and rain are the ingredients for growth, and God makes sure everyone gets their fair share—even when God is displeased with their growth trajectory. But why? Why waste resources on unproductive and undeserving people and situations? Why should good things happen to bad people? Because God believes that bad people, when given the right opportunity and care, can choose to be good people! That is great news for all of us less-than-perfect individuals.

Question: Upon whom do you need to shower more of your time, attention, and care?

Practice: Pick a family member, a neighbor, or a colleague whom you dislike or consistently judge. Take a moment today to pray for them. Do not pray for them to change more to your liking, just pray for their well-being, their blessing, their flourishing. Pay attention to what happens within you as you pray generously for their wellness.

Prayer: Lord, I don't like wasting my time and effort on people and situations that appear unproductive. Why should I spend time with a troublesome employee? Why should I further commit myself to my spouse when the relationship seems to be going nowhere? Why should I work hard for a boss who does not give me the credit or the compensation I deserve? Lord, help me grasp the truth that you do more than hold out hope for those who fall short of your glory. You give everyone exactly what they need to grow and mature into good, faithful, compassionate people. Thank you, Lord God. In your name, I pray. Amen.

DAY 17

Practicing Piety

Beware of practicing your piety before others in order to be seen by them;
for then you have no reward from your Father in heaven. So whenever you
give alms, do not sound a trumpet before you, as the hypocrites do in the
synagogues and in the streets, so that they may be praised by others. Truly I
tell you, they have received their reward. But when you give alms, do not let
your left hand know what your right hand is doing, so that your alms may
be done in secret; and your Father who sees in secret will reward you. And
whenever you pray, do not be like the hypocrites; for they love to stand and
pray in the synagogues and at the street corners, so that they may be seen
by others. Truly I tell you, they have received their reward. But whenever
you pray, go into your room and shut the door and pray to your Father
who is in secret; and your Father who sees in secret will reward you.

MATTHEW 6:1-6

Reflection: Piety, the faithful and regular devotion to religious
practice, is to be done in private. Commitment to almsgiving and
prayer—generosity to others and conversation with God—are acts
to be done without fanfare or recognition. Faith practices that are
meant to cultivate and deepen our relationship with God are not
engaged in for personal recognition. This teaching can seem out
of time and place in communities and countries that have grown

quite self-conscious and uncomfortable with the public display of spiritual practice. However, there are many cultures and peoples for whom religious observance is a public act, where personal piety is rewarded with respect and praise.

Jesus clearly witnessed in his own culture and community a proclivity to engage in elaborate demonstrations of faith and piety, and he believed it was a cause for concern. Jesus knew that even good and purposeful acts and activities of faith could be perverted by using them to raise one's profile or persona. According to Jesus, private piety was a more faithful and effective way to connect an individual with God, thus avoiding the temptation toward religious pomp and pride.

While public acts of religious piety might not be as commonplace for us as they were in first-century Judaism, civic acts of generosity might be just as spiritually perilous. We live in an age and culture where gifts of significance come with naming rights, and donors great and small expect to be recognized for their philanthropic interests and acts. We all have within us the desire to put on a good show for others to see—even, and perhaps especially, if the way we conduct ourselves in private is less than holy and good. According to the introduction to this section of teaching, Jesus is not entirely opposed to public prayer and almsgiving, though he is concerned when the motivation for acts of piety is the desire to be seen by others. And because we all have tendencies to want to be noticed for the good and godly behaviors we occasionally exhibit, Jesus encourages us to practice our faith quietly, anonymously, secretly to avoid the sins of self-aggrandizement and pride.

Question: When you make a gift, why do you like being recognized for it?

Practice: Make an anonymous and generous donation this week to a cause or organization you care about. Or, offer a gift to someone in need without their awareness of the donation's origin. Do good for goodness's sake, not in order to be recognized.

Practicing What Jesus Preached

Prayer: Lord, my prayers might be in private, but when I do a good work I like to be recognized for it. I know that I desire to look better to others than you know me to be. I want to put on a good show in public, particularly if I am not proud of who I am in private. Lord, help my private actions to be more faithful, and my public efforts to be motivated more by service than pride. In your name, I pray. Amen.

How to Pray

When you are praying, do not heap up empty phrases as the Gentiles do; for they think that they will be heard because of their many words. Do not be like them, for your Father knows what you need before you ask him. Pray then in this way: Our Father in heaven, hallowed be your name. Your kingdom come. Your will be done, on earth as it is in heaven. Give us this day our daily bread. And forgive us our debts, as we also have forgiven our debtors. And do not bring us to the time of trial, but rescue us from the evil one. For if you forgive others their trespasses, your heavenly Father will also forgive you; but if you do not forgive others, neither will your Father forgive your trespasses.

MATTHEW 6:7–15

Reflection: Prayer is an honest conversation with God. We are meant to express ourselves to the Lord, and we are to take time to listen. Conversation—human and divine—is a two-way discourse. Rhythms of speaking and silence are essential to the practice of prayer. When a person is seasoned in prayer, this practice of communication with God can flow rather easily and effortlessly even if the content of the discussion is difficult and painful. But prayer is not something we are born knowing how to do. We might be aware of an internal longing for the divine from an early age, but the practice of communication with God must be taught and learned if one is to practice prayer as a regular discipline.

Prayer was a priority for Jesus. In the Gospels, Jesus regularly stole away from the crowds that pursued him to engage in private discourse with God, a practice he encouraged his followers to ascribe to. In this passage, Jesus taught his disciples to pray—Jesus gave them a specific form to follow and words to say. Jesus' instructions were clear and direct. Pray in secret. Don't practice your piety to impress others. Don't offer wordy, effusive prayers. Speak simply. Trust that God knows what you need before you speak, but pray anyway. Always pray for forgiveness, and put your prayer into action by forgiving others. For Jesus, prayer should be intimate and concise, and prompt us to deal with others as we have requested that God deal with us. This might all be a way of saying to his disciples—and to us all—don't overthink, just pray.

The idea that one does not need to be particularly creative in prayer is borne out in Jesus' own life and ministry. There are numerous examples in the Gospels of Jesus quoting Psalms, particularly when he was in danger or in a moment of crisis. The Psalms are the prayers of the Jewish people, and the collection we are familiar with in our Bibles would have served as something of a prayer book for Jesus. Jesus knew these ancient prayers so well, that when he encountered a particular situation, he could call to mind a specific prayer that he would recite. The act of speaking to God, even, perhaps especially, reciting an ancient prayer and meditating on the words of the prayer itself, are an effective means of conversation and communion with the Lord.

Question: What are obstacles preventing you from praying more regularly?

Practice: Memorize one psalm of any length. Recite that psalm to yourself as a prayer in the morning and in the evening, as Jesus would have done.

Prayer: Lord, hear my prayer. In my speaking, in my reciting, in my openness, and in my silence; hear my prayer. In morning light and as dusk darkens to night, hear my prayer. Hear my prayer, and allow me to hear you speaking back. In your name, I pray. Amen.

Essential and Neglected Discipline

And whenever you fast, do not look dismal, like the hypocrites, for they disfigure their faces so as to show others that they are fasting. Truly I tell you, they have received their reward. But when you fast, put oil on your head and wash your face, so that your fasting may be seen not by others but by your Father who is in secret; and your Father who sees in secret will reward you.

MATTHEW 6:16-18

Reflection: Jesus' focus on the practice of fasting continues his theme of practicing piety in private and highlights the value of fasting as a spiritual discipline. The Bible indicates that as a sign of repentance, people were supposed to refrain from eating, and sit in sackcloth and ashes. This was a visible act of "humiliation," the term and practice of humbling oneself before God employed by Hebrew people of faith. Jesus' discourse on fasting was an admonition to engage in less observable forms and expressions of penance.

However, Jesus' attention to the spiritual practice of "going without" is an opportunity to consider this essential, yet often neglected, discipline. Fasting is abstinence from consumption. Fasting is the discipline of confronting the lusts and longings within us that tend to crowd out space for the holy. Fasting is an opportunity to deal with the impulse to mask our deepest needs with passing pleasures.

Many of us live lives of unchecked and unquestioned consumption. We have an economy built upon, and fueled by, consumption. We are told that the growth of our economy and the goodness of life can be measured by consumer activity and consumer confidence. There are whole industries that exist to promote and facilitate our consumptive appetites. Unfortunately, the consuming and overconsuming of food, material goods, entertainment, information, social media, and so very much more, has become a way of life for us. In fact, we hardly give a second thought to the impulses that lie underneath our seemingly insatiable appetites. Therefore, the call to restrict ourselves has become something of an anathema to our way of life.

Of all the spiritual disciplines that we might engage in today, the practice of fasting could be the most essential for healthy living, vital relationships, and dynamic faith. Less really is more. When we consume less, we have more time and space for the activities and relationships that have been created by God to be the most satisfying part of life. A call to fasting is an opportunity to stop stuffing ourselves with empty promises and unneeded products, while being open and available to that which God wants to share with us and grow within us.

Question: What do you consume too much of—alcohol, food, websurfing, pornography, social media, purchasing, or something else?

Practice: For the next week, fast from an impulse that you know is unhealthy for you. Abstain from nonessential purchases, or refrain from snacking between meals. Significantly limit your screen time. Avoid digital distractions by turning off your media or communication alerts.

Prayer: Lord, you know that too many of my lusts and longings are out of control. I consume and consume, mindlessly, until my waistline grows, and my calendar is completely booked, and my spending is overextended. Grant me the courage to set limits and commit to those boundaries. Help me to engage in a spiritual discipline of fasting, so that my life becomes less cluttered with addictions and impulses that get in the way of our relationship. And, Lord, when I falter in my commitments, allow me to shake off the failure and begin again. I want less cluttering my life, and more of you! In Jesus' name, I pray. Amen.

A Following Heart

*Do not store up for yourselves treasures on earth, where moth
and rust consume and where thieves break in and steal; but
store up for yourselves treasures in heaven, where neither moth
nor rust consumes and where thieves do not break in and steal.
For where your treasure is, there your heart will be also.*

MATTHEW 6:19–21

Reflection: This brief text is a go-to stewardship Scripture often
employed to guilt people into giving more money to the church.
It is used as a way of saying, *"If you really cared, if you really loved
Jesus, if your heart were in the right place, you would be more generous in your giving."* There is no question that Jesus cared about our
relationship with money. He preached and taught about it often.
However, Jesus' interest in money had to do with his understanding that our love for money can get in the way of love of God and
neighbor. In fact, we often endow financial resources with the
power and influence that should be reserved for God alone. We
tend to think that enough money can protect us, sustain us, and
make us happy. We believe a robust bank account, a diverse stock
portfolio, enough life insurance and retirement savings is our path
to salvation. Because our trust in God is often supplanted by our

reliance on financial resources, Jesus was always encouraging his followers to have a healthy relationship with money—make it, but don't love it; use it, but don't worship it.

However, in this Scripture, if you look closely, you will not find an admonition for greater generosity, but rather a strategic way of investing ourselves so that we are prompted to engage in more meaningful pursuits and relationships. While it is tempting to interpret this passage of Scripture as meaning that what you fund is what you care about, the ordering of the passage does not support that emphasis. This memorable text suggests that if you want your heart to be in a new place, invest your resources in that location. Place your treasure, your time, and your talents where you want your heart to wind up. When thoughtfully considered, your checkbook and your calendar can help to facilitate a set of new and better priorities in your life—because your heart has a way of following your treasure. This is an extraordinarily helpful and liberating understanding of the power of financial resources! If you know what you want to do and be to the glory of God, start investing yourself and your money in that direction. Make a financial commitment in the direction you feel called to go, and Jesus asserts that your life will follow. You don't need to fall into the trap of deciding you can become truly generous once you have figured out your direction in life. You can actually influence your direction in life by investing in advance of yourself. Put your money where you feel called to be, and you will get there!

Question: Where do you want your heart to be?

Practice: Review your bank and credit card statements. Are you using your resources in ways that are satisfying to you and pleasing to God? If not, what investment can you make in your future? Go online and select a class you would like to take, or a conference you would like to attend, or a lecturer you would like to go to hear. Register yourself.

Prayer: Lord, where do you want me to invest myself in the future? Let me know. Encourage me to take a leap of faith and pour my resources in the direction you want me to go. In Jesus' name, I pray. Amen.

What Catches Our Eye

The eye is the lamp of the body. So, if your eye is healthy, your whole body will be full of light; but if your eye is unhealthy, your whole body will be full of darkness. If then the light in you is darkness, how great is the darkness!

MATTHEW 6:22-23

Reflection: It is interesting to note what catches our eye. When we are considering purchasing a particular car, suddenly we see similar vehicles on the road everywhere we go. When we hear about a viral video, or tweet, or Facebook post, we go online to watch and add to the "views." When we are feverishly looking for a sign from God, we take note of birds in the air, or billboards we pass, or messages we receive from strangers as if they potentially convey a word from the Almighty. This expresses the truth that when we are paying attention and focused on looking for something, there is no telling what we will actually see—whether real or imagined.

Our world is so very visual. Advertising agencies, marketing teams, and public relations firms know if they can catch our eye they have a shot at grabbing our attention. Words, slogans, images assail us from every angle imaginable—print media, broadcast media, and social media call out to us to look, to see, and behold. Of course, there is the even more shadowy side of our visual proclivities that take the form of viewing pornography, or voraciously reading heated and hateful message board threads, or simply rubbernecking on the road—or in life—to slowly witness the accidental misfortune of others.

In this section of his sermon, Jesus seems to be saying that how we view life gives shape to who we are. Our sight and insight determine our overall health and relational wellness. What we take in visually has a way of forming us internally. If our eyes are healthy—meaning that we look upon that which is good and holy and redemptive—God's light shines through us. If we focus on that which is unhealthy, sinful, divisive, the light within us is diminished until darkness overtakes us and engulfs our lives. We were made to be a lamp of God shining forth into the world; we were not formed to perpetuate the darkness that existed before creation.

Question: If you desire to receive signs from God, where might you need to focus your attention more? Where should you focus less?

Practice: Be mindful and discriminating about what you see and view. Instead of endlessly surfing the internet and social media, read a good and inspiring book. Instead of shopping on a street full of alluring signs that encourage consumption, take a quiet walk in the woods and behold God's creation. Instead of looking covetously at all that your family, friends, or neighbors have, pause and give thanks to God for all the blessings God has entrusted to you.

Prayer: Lord, help me to fix my eyes and my heart on that which is good, holy, and meaningful. Help me to focus on the blessings of life so that the light of gratitude and grace can shine through me. Keep my eyes from darkness and help me to view life as you do . . . with faith, hope, and love. In your name, I pray. Amen.

Choosing Masters

No one can serve two masters; for a slave will either hate
the one and love the other, or be devoted to the one and
despise the other. You cannot serve God and wealth.

MATTHEW 6:24

Reflection: If we choose to be honest with ourselves and the Lord, we have to admit that we often have divided loyalties. We commit ourselves to a whole host of competing relationships—interpersonal, vocational, psychological. There are certain people, specific responsibilities, personal histories, and even various addictions that can gain mastery over us. Sometimes, perhaps oftentimes, our devotions build over time, subtly, little by little, until we realize we have become indentured or even enslaved to one or more powers in our lives. We discover that work is our ruler, or a dysfunctional personal relationship binds us, or an emotional injury from our past keeps forcing us to make poor decisions. Or we discover that our lusts and longings drive our days. The unchecked desire for affirmation, the want of love and intimacy, the craving for power or control runs and eventual ruins our lives. To have and maintain a healthy prioritization of the competing influences in our lives, we must first admit that we have many masters.

While Jesus rightfully points out our conflicted and conflicting commitments—naming the fact that being bound to multiple masters leads to envy and animosity—Jesus also asserts we have a choice. We can choose who or what we serve. We have agency to decide where we will place our loyalties. Jesus wants us to choose well, and to choose God. That means, of course, placing our relationship with God before and above other relationships, which is not always our first instinct. If primary devotion is offered to something or someone other than our omniscient, omnipresent, and eternal God, our lives will not be as expansive and impactful as they might be. Being a good parent, being a faithful spouse, being an encouraging and hardworking employer or employee is not at all bad, but even good commitments can become limited and limiting if they are our first priority and primary devotion. When God is our chosen master—when the love of God reigns in our lives—healthy relationships, meaningful work, and healthy habits naturally follow.

While Jesus' teaching on masters and mastery has broad implications for us, we do need to take note that Jesus aims squarely at the target of money . . . *again*. Jesus taught about right relationship with money with great regularity. It is because, as previously mentioned, financial resources and our pursuit of them often displace our devotion to the Lord. Mammon—the trappings of wealth—can falsely fill us with a sense of security that only our eternal and everlasting God can truly offer. Money and wealth are not bad in and of themselves. In fact, affluence affords individuals the opportunity to make a significant and positive impact on others. However, serving money, being devoted to it, or giving it mastery over us can be unhealthy and destructive. As Jesus will go on to illustrate in his sermon, devotion to God, and working for and in service of God's kingdom, will allow for a sense of solace and security that nothing and no one else in the world can provide.

Question: What are ways your loyalties are divided?

Practice: Take a piece of US paper currency, and highlight the words "In God We Trust." Keep that bill in your purse or wallet.

Do not spend it, but look at it when you go to make purchases. When you go to make a payment, notice the highlighted words, and consider where your trust is ultimately placed.

Prayer: Lord, I render service to so many masters other than you. I care about you, I love you, I want to be more deeply connected to you, but my devotions and dedication speak a different truth. Help me to gain a degree of distance this week from the people, engagements, and addictions that consume my time and my life, leaving little left over for you. Allow me to make you and our relationship a priority in my life. You are my Lord and my God, I desire to serve you and no other. In your name, I pray. Amen.

Do Not Worry

Therefore I tell you, do not worry about your life, what you will eat or what you will drink, or about your body, what you will wear. Is not life more than food, and the body more than clothing? Look at the birds of the air; they neither sow nor reap nor gather into barns, and yet your heavenly Father feeds them. Are you not of more value than they? And can any of you by worrying add a single hour to your span of life? And why do you worry about clothing? Consider the lilies of the field, how they grow; they neither toil nor spin, yet I tell you, even Solomon in all his glory was not clothed like one of these. But if God so clothes the grass of the field, which is alive today and tomorrow is thrown into the oven, will he not much more clothe you—you of little faith? Therefore do not worry, saying, "What will we eat?" or "What will we drink?" or "What will we wear?" for it is the Gentiles who strive for all these things; and indeed your heavenly Father knows that you need all these things. But strive first for the kingdom of God and his righteousness, and all these things will be given to you as well. So do not worry about tomorrow, for tomorrow will bring worries of its own. Today's trouble is enough for today.

MATTHEW 6:25-34

Reflection: To follow Jesus means to dismiss anxiety. *"Do not worry," "Fear not," "Be not be afraid,"* are versions of one of the most common and consistent commands in the Bible. The frequency of these commands seems to indicate that worry, stress, and anxiety have been plaguing the human spirit for a very long time. Of course, simply telling—or commanding—chronically anxious people not to worry is not particularly helpful. In fact, when we have something we are deeply concerned about—well-founded or not—being told not to stress about it can be acutely annoying. An admonition not to worry can actually seem dismissive of one's concerns. But Jesus' fairly extensive teaching about worry is not merely an attempt to ease anxiety—it is an encouragement to trust.

Don't worry, *trust God,* is the divine imperative for our earthly living. As sermon illustrations, Jesus pointed out the constancy and provision in the created order. Consider the birds of the air and the flowers in the field—they have everything they need, and they do not seem beset by stress. If God can take care of all of creation, trust that the Lord can take care of you. So, Jesus' teaching isn't dismissive of worry nor chastising of needless anxiety—it is an encouragement to trust that the Lord of the universe can supply what you need.

Jesus does, however, make a suggestion that ventures beyond trust *to action.* Jesus offers one of the best antidotes to anxiety. Stress and worry have a way of paralyzing us, whereas meaningful work gets us moving. Activity is Jesus' suggested antidote to anxiety. *"Strive first for the kingdom of God and his righteousness,"* is the way Jesus phrased it. Don't worry, work for the kingdom. Don't live fearfully, live righteously. Don't get anxious, just actively do the work of God in the world . . . and everything else will fall into place. Jesus says you can take your mind off your worries by fully engaging in God's work. If you have ever tried it, you know it is true. The antidote to fretful anxiety is righteous activity!

Question: What worries you most?

Practice: When you begin to sense that worry is crowding your mind—choose to get active instead. Exercise. Make a meal for your family. Call a friend out of the blue to see how they are doing. Volunteer for a day of service or a mission trip with your school, employer, or church.

Prayer: Lord, when I sit idly, I find myself easily ensnared by worry. When I get active, and pursue the righteousness you call me to, anxiety has a way of dissolving from my heart and mind. Help me to occupy my mind and my life with your work so that my living doesn't get overcome by my worry. Help me to trust in you. In your name, I pray. Amen.

Judgmentalism

Do not judge, so that you may not be judged. For with the judgment
you make you will be judged, and the measure you give will be the
measure you get. Why do you see the speck in your neighbor's eye, but
do not notice the log in your own eye? Or how can you say to your
neighbor, "Let me take the speck out of your eye," while the log is in
your own eye? You hypocrite, first take the log out of your own eye, and
then you will see clearly to take the speck out of your neighbor's eye.

MATTHEW 7:1-5

Reflection: We judge people all the time. We are quick to criti-
cize, and our critique is often unflinchingly harsh. While sensible
people need to make judgments all the time—weighing choices
which need to be made, evaluating opportunities and obstacles,
discerning right from wrong in a world where ambiguity often
abounds—our propensity for judgment can quickly devolve into
judgmentalism. Sound judgment is essential for faithful and successful living. Fair assessment and good choices are activities that
tend to build up and are constructive. However, judgmentalism—
critique of others without a hint of charity, generosity, or grace—
tears down and is inherently destructive in nature. Judgmentalism
can become habitual. We can become ruthlessly critical without

even realizing how damaging we are being. We can get to a place where we critique others as if we were entirely above reproach.

Jesus made a startling comment in this section of his sermon that has the ability to convict and correct each of us who are less than charitable in our critique of others. Jesus said: "For with the judgment you make you will be judged, and the measure you give will be the measure you get." That is about as unsettling a comment as Jesus could make. Jesus asserts that God will judge us with the same measure we use to critique others. If we are merciless in our examination and condemnation of others, we should expect the same treatment from God. If we think about how we tend to evaluate others, the idea that God will treat us similarly should give us significant pause. However, there is a flip side to that understanding that should be considered. Jesus is also telling us if we are generous and thoughtful in our assessment of others, God will be equally gracious with us. Jesus offers us a stinging rebuke, while at the same time, issuing us a wonderful opportunity. We get to set the bar for our own evaluation from God! We get to choose. Will our judgments and God's be severe or forgiving?

Finally, as he often does, Jesus offers us a substitute practice for our judgmentalism. Jesus didn't merely say "do not judge." Jesus went on to offer an activity that can replace our impulse to critique others. Instead of focusing on the faults and failings of others, start working on yourself. Deal with your own stuff. Grapple with your own issues. Take the log out of your own eye before you try to examine the fleck of imperfection in others. In short, leave the judging to God and get to work on yourself. That is sound and sensible advice that can get us out of the hurtful habit of judgmentalism!

Question: Whom do you judge? And how harsh are your judgments?

Practice: Ask someone you trust where they see need for growth in your life.

Prayer: Lord, who made me the judge of other people? No one! You are the judge, I am not. Keep me in my place. Help me to focus on my own issues while leaving the evaluation to you. Encourage in me a graciousness toward others that I will hope and pray you will apply to me. In Jesus' name, I pray. Amen.

Precious as Pearls

*Do not give what is holy to dogs; and do not throw your pearls before
swine, or they will trample them under foot and turn and maul you.*

MATTHEW 7:6

Reflection: While Jesus' lessons for us are exacting and his expectations are high, it is clear that Jesus' teachings are motivated by love
and commitment to each of us. Jesus spoke to a crowd of people—
and by extension us—and said, "You are as precious as pearls." "You
are of great value." "What you have to offer the world is of excep-
tional worth." Sometimes when someone is offering us rigorous
guidance, as Jesus does in his sermon, it can feel like punishment or
rebuke. What we must always bear in mind is that throughout the
Bible God offers us guidance, instruction, and commandments out
of a deep love for us and a desire for us to live well.

It is curious, and perhaps quite intentional, that this section of
teaching follows Jesus' caution to us about uncharitably critiquing
others. After admonishing us to get to work on ourselves before
examining others (extract the logs in our own eyes before looking
to pick the specks out of others), Jesus offers this note about our inherent value. The audience for Jesus' sermon was deeply influenced
by Hebrew, Roman, and Hellenistic cultural understandings; and

the use of the image of a pearl would have called to mind a number of complementary symbols. For the Greeks, pearls were of unrivaled value and were closely associated with loving commitment between two parties. For the Romans, pearls were considered the primary symbol of wealth and social standing. For the Jews of Jesus' day, pearls were considered exceedingly rare, and unique because they did not require cutting or polishing to be treasured. This means that God, as communicated through Jesus, considers us of great value, has deep love and commitment for us, and does not need anything added to us or taken from us in order for us to be treasured.

To God, we are treasured possessions who should be aware of our value—not prideful of our value—but cognizant of our inherent worth. Therefore, we should not be careless with ourselves and what we offer the world. Who you are, what you do, and what you have to offer are of great value, so do not spend or expend yourself carelessly. Do not commit yourself in relationship with someone who is abusive to you. Do not allow an employer or organization to grind out of you your sense of worth. Do not allow your own self-critical nature to become a belittling influence in your life. You were created as a pearl. You are loved. You are of supreme value. You were uniquely crafted, and do not need to be anything other than what God has made you, to be beautiful, whole, and complete. You were made as an adornment for God, not as a doormat for the world. Believe it for yourself. See it in others.

Question: How would it change your outlook and attitude to truly believe you are a pearl of great value?

Practice: Take a moment today to tell a person close to you why they are precious to you. Be specific.

Prayer: Lord, while I may be prone to be careless and overly harsh in my critique of others, I am also less than generous with myself. I am aware of my sinfulness, my shortcomings, and my failures. Honestly, it is difficult to understand and even more challenging to accept the possibility that you find me to be dearly beloved. And yet, I will try to take Jesus at his word, and consider who I am, and what I do, to be precious in your sight. I will try to receive the sense of value you place on me, so that I can hold that same perspective of others . . . as you desire. In Jesus' name, I pray. Amen.

Persistence

Ask, and it will be given you; search, and you will find; knock, and the door will be opened for you. For everyone who asks receives, and everyone who searches finds, and for everyone who knocks, the door will be opened. Is there anyone among you who, if your child asks for bread, will give a stone? Or if the child asks for a fish, will give a snake? If you then, who are evil, know how to give good gifts to your children, how much more will your Father in heaven give good things to those who ask him!

MATTHEW 7:7–11

Reflection: Oftentimes faith is hard. God seems silent and distant. Jesus can appear to be an idealized character from the past. And the winds of the Holy Spirit can seem to have completely stilled. Our faith can feel anemic and our God unresponsive. Everyone— even the most thoroughly devout people—has seasons when faith falters and connection with the Lord seems to fail. Those seasons can last for days, months, even years. The first thing to know is that "not feeling the faith" is a natural part of our journey as human beings with an internal, but not always consistent, draw to the Divine.

One of the primary reasons God can seem far away from us, and our faith less than fervent, is the level of effort we put into the relationship. Without question, God must, and does, bear much responsibility for our relationship, but we need to be active participants in making the connection. Sometimes, we put off matters of faith until we feel we have the time to commit to the effort. Other times, we are so busy, we don't make the time for prayer, scriptural study, fellowship, and worship that are tried and true avenues for the Spirit to gain access to us. We might even let anger and anxiety so overtake us that there isn't much room for the Lord in the midst of the angst that engulfs our soul.

In this portion of Jesus' sermon, he encourages us to keep up the effort to connect with God, and promises that those efforts will ultimately be rewarded. Ask. Search. Knock. Do the work of faith. Pray. Study. Worship. He tells us that if we keep making an effort to connect, the Lord will respond. Just as a faithful parent can be counted on to provide for beloved children, Jesus says that the Lord will respond to our needs when we seek him out and ask. If we are persistent each day in our asking, searching, and knocking, we will find that the connection with God we long for, the relationship with the Lord we desire, and the sense of the Spirit we crave has been available to us all along. You may not get everything you want, but you will discover the relationship you most need.

Question: Parents do not always give children what they ask for. Can you think of reasons God would not give you exactly what you want when you want it?

Practice: Pick something important in your life that you really need. Not a want, but a true need. Every morning and every night add that request to your prayers. Be blunt and direct with God. Ask. Seek. Knock. Keep at that specific practice for the next week, offering up the very same prayer every time you bow your head and bend your knee. Be sure to add words of gratitude for what the Lord has already provided you. Take note of how the Lord responds to you.

Prayer: Lord, first and foremost, thank you for all you have given to me. I want to thank you even, and perhaps especially, for the longing for you within me that prompts my desire to seek you out. My hunger for faith and my desire to be in your presence is indeed a gift. Thank you. Lord, there are specific requests I want to make of you. There are things I feel I need for life to feel full and whole and complete. And yet, I realize what I want and what you know I need might be quite different. Draw close to me. Hear my cries. Respond to my searching. Answer when I knock. For if I were to list all I desire in life, that which I crave the most is intimacy and immediacy of relationship with you. In Jesus' name, I pray. Amen.

Simple

In everything do to others as you would have them do to you; for this is the law and the prophets.

MATTHEW 7:12

Reflection: Life can be complicated. Relational and vocational dilemmas abound. We have concerns about our health, our finances, our friends and family. Much of the time we feel lost and uncertain about what path we are to take and what direction in life we are to go. We would like to believe that we can navigate life by simply doing what is right and good and just. But we know that decisions and the situations before us are seldom as easy as choosing between what is right and what is wrong. The world is not clear-cut, full of black-and-white questions to be asked and answered. There are so many shades of gray, and we often find ourselves having to choose between multiple good outcomes and options, or between the lesser of two or more evils.

However, according to Jesus, while life is complicated, our living doesn't have to be. Jesus said that to live according to the will of God, all we need to do is treat other people as we would like to be treated. In every challenging decision and difficult circumstance in which we find ourselves, we can simply ask ourselves how we would like to be regarded, spoken to, cared for, and then we can act accordingly. If we treat others with the respect, dignity, and compassion we desire, then perhaps we will find a way forward in life that is not so stressful and confusing. This is not being simplistic, because knowing what to do can be easier than actually doing what is right. However, knowing the correct way to live may just be as simple as Jesus suggests. When you find yourself in a difficult situation, ask yourself how you would like to be treated, and respond in kind. The answer to that basic, yet profound question, fulfills the "law and the prophets." In other words, doing to others as you would have them do to you, fulfills all the commands God has asked us to live by. Simple.

Question: How would you feel if God treated you the way you treat God?

Practice: In every interaction you have today, pause to consider how you appreciate being spoken to, cared for, and encouraged. Do likewise to others.

Prayer: Lord, life feels complicated and challenging . . . and, in truth, there are times when I just feel downright overwhelmed. I realize, however, that I might be making too much of the difficult situations and relationships I find myself in. What if I based all my decisions and actions on how I would like to be treated? What if I fulfilled your will by simply doing as you ask? Life can be hard, but perhaps my living doesn't have to be. For this I pray, in your name. Amen.

DAY 28

Gates and Roadways

Enter through the narrow gate; for the gate is wide and the road is easy that leads to destruction, and there are many who take it. For the gate is narrow and the road is hard that leads to life, and there are few who find it.

MATTHEW 7:13-14

Reflection: As we age and life experience piles upon us, there is a revelation that often dawns on us: many of the best things in life take a lot of time, effort, and patience. Relationships, for instance, are incredibly taxing and yet the most profound of blessings. Our relationship with a spouse, our relationships with children and grandchildren, our relationships with friends, and even our relationship with work and hobbies, if we choose to do them well, are blessings beyond compare. But each and every one of our relationships—interpersonal, vocational, spiritual—requires intense effort. Like squeezing oneself through a narrow gate no bigger than the eye of a needle, or like trekking up a winding mountain road with no pinnacle in sight, truly life-giving relationships and activities are demanding enterprises.

And in truth, we all tire at some point or other, and long for an easier path to the fulfillment and joy we seek. When the marriage gets difficult, we consider quitting and moving on. When the job doesn't feel satisfying, we consider quitting and moving on. When the school we are in, or the friend groups we have been a part of, or the associations we participate in, demand more than we feel like contributing, we consider quitting and moving on. Every single one of us has times when we prefer to choose the wide gate and the easy road. It is natural. Yet we know that the guilty pleasures we engage in, and the manageable goals we set for ourselves, and the ease of minimal commitment, are not ultimately fulfilling.

To be challenged offers us the opportunity to be changed in important ways. To have to truly strive for a goal makes the success of accomplishment all the more satisfying. To face obstacles head-on allows us to learn that we can, by God's grace, overcome whatever challenges are before us. It can be an incredible accomplishment and a great joy to celebrate a fifty-year anniversary when you considered ending the relationship at year five. It can be an incredible accomplishment and a great joy when you spend most of your career in one organization, instead of hopping from job to job every time you get annoyed or bored. It can be an incredible accomplishment and a great joy when you choose to invest deeply in the community where you live, instead of uprooting every few years in search of greener pastures.

Narrow gates and rough roads tend to require a commitment to fidelity, patience, and discipline. But a gate is a passageway, not a destination; and a road is for traveling, not settling. All gates and roads lead somewhere—they are not ends in themselves. Therefore, the hardship of every good journey does not last forever, but the joy experienced upon arrival can define and last a lifetime, and beyond.

Question: What aspects of following Jesus do you find particularly challenging? Why?

Practice: Take a walk or hike of a length and rigor that exceeds your norm. Select a phrase from Scripture, or a word that represents a virtue you would like reflected in your life. As you trek, speak the word or phrase quietly to yourself. Match the rhythm of your speaking with the rhythm of your walking.

Prayer: Lord, there are so many times when I want to quit, give up, and throw in the towel. Life is hard, relationships are difficult, and there are obstacles and challenges before me that appear insurmountable. There are times in my life when I just want to take it easy, and for the gates before me to open without so much effort. And yet, Lord, I know that the most important parts of my life are the ones that have required the most and the best of my efforts. Help me in my fatigue. Encourage me to take the right road and to enter through the correct gate no matter the difficulty incurred. I want life, and life in abundance, as you promise. Allow me the resolve to put in the effort to get there. In your name, I pray. Amen.

DAY 29

Good Fruit

Beware of false prophets, who come to you in sheep's clothing but inwardly are ravenous wolves. You will know them by their fruits. Are grapes gathered from thorns, or figs from thistles? In the same way, every good tree bears good fruit, but the bad tree bears bad fruit. A good tree cannot bear bad fruit, nor can a bad tree bear good fruit. Every tree that does not bear good fruit is cut down and thrown into the fire. Thus you will know them by their fruits.

MATTHEW 7:15-20

Reflection: Most of us are filled with good intentions. We don't start our day planning how we can cut corners, lie, or fill people with unreasonable expectations. Most of us begin by desiring to live honestly, truthfully, and with integrity. But as the day wears on we are pressed, pushed, and pressured in a myriad of directions. By day's end we have said things we didn't mean, we have made promises we don't know how we will keep, and we have made decisions that are not in line with our best intentions.

Like Jesus' caution about sin throughout his sermon, his remarks are stark and jarring. Reading his words can give us the impression that people are either bad or good, wrong or right, demons or angels. However, life experience has taught us that we are all a mixture of good intentions and less-than-pure motives.

Unlike the old westerns that adorned the good guys with white hats and the bad guys with black . . . we live and work and act in a world shrouded by ambiguity. The best of us have moments when we are overcome by anger, resentment, rage, and a thousand other harmful impulses. Likewise, the most depraved of sinners have moments when they show something of a divine spark within them. Jesus understood this. His closest students and friends were faithful *and* flawed. They could stand firm in one moment and scatter the next. They could call Jesus "Lord" in one breath, and call him "stranger" in the next. The disciple who could offer praise, could also betray. Jesus knew that all people are made up of mixed motives and conflicting interests.

In this sermon Jesus says that intentions and impulses do not mean as much as our actions. There is no debate, according to Jesus' earlier address, that impure thoughts and imaginings are harmful and damaging, and can lead to disastrous ramifications. But here, Jesus shifts to indicate that our ideas and instincts do not amount to much until we put them into practice. We are not ultimately judged by what we thought about doing, or by what we intended to do, or by what we planned to refrain from doing. We are known not by the promise of our lives, but by the product of our lives. In the end, we are judged by what we have produced— our fruit.

Question: Do you bear good fruit in your living, working, and acting?

Practice: As a way of understanding the process of bearing fruit, do one of the following: work in a garden. Buy a plant and care for it. Pause, and in gratitude for God's abundance and creativity, take a closer look at all the amazing and unique fruits and vegetables in your grocery store.

Prayer: Lord, I am indeed filled with good intentions, but I find I am often hard pressed to follow through on them. It is not so much that I feel like a bad person, but I do feel like a person who thinks better than I act. Help me to produce good fruit. Help me to convert good intentions into good actions. Help me to build a legacy of good work in your world. In Jesus' name, I pray. Amen.

Willful

Not everyone who says to me, "Lord, Lord," will enter the kingdom of heaven, but only the one who does the will of my Father in heaven. On that day many will say to me, "Lord, Lord, did we not prophesy in your name, and cast out demons in your name, and do many deeds of power in your name?" Then I will declare to them, "I never knew you; go away from me, you evildoers."

MATTHEW 7:21–23

Reflection: Proclaiming oneself a Christian—a follower of Jesus—does not mean that is who one truly is. Right belief does not ensure eternal acceptance. We can speak the correct words, we can even perform impressive and heroic acts of faith, but unless we discover and do the will of God we miss the mark. This instruction seems both harsh and confusing. How can we say the right words, believe the right thing, and even do powerful works of faith and not be accepted or acceptable to Jesus? As unsettling as these statements by Jesus might be, Jesus touches on a critique of contemporary Christianity and present-day Christians we are all too familiar with: *hypocrisy*. We don't practice what we preach, and we don't preach what Jesus actually taught. We identify Jesus as "Lord." We call him "Savior." We may even recognize Jesus as "Son of God." But we too often fail to follow his instruction, and God's will. We take on the name Christian—perhaps even proudly—but choose to live out our faith in our own way, picking and choosing the commands that are of interest to us, while discarding those we dislike or find too onerous.

We know well the failures and fallings of pastoral leaders in the contemporary church. The church of Jesus too often makes news today because of philandering megachurch pastors, or pedophile priests, or faith-healing evangelists who deceive the masses for profit. There are a lot of Christians, and much Christian living, that diverge from the hard and holy work Jesus calls us to. While high-profile scandal captures headlines, we do not need to look much further than our own lives to understand the basis for Jesus' caution. Our daily living speaks louder than many of our professions of faith. And when we talk better than we act, our faith can appear hypocritical.

The will of God is not primarily done by an eloquent profession of faith, nor by impressive works to be seen and admired by all. Our faith and devotion to Jesus is best witnessed in daily actions that align with God's desires for us. Being salt and light. Honoring the vows we have made to others. Resisting the sin within us, while praying for those who do evil in the world. Forsaking worry, while patiently working for the kingdom. Avoiding the harsh critique of others, and treating people the way we wish to be treated ourselves. Grand and impressive professions and acts of faith are not what please Jesus most. Simple, daily, faithful living is what leads to our salvation—here and now, and on into eternity!

Question: Do you talk better than you act? Why?

Practice: Look back over the previous suggestions for faith practice. Select one practice you really struggled to adhere to. Try practicing it again.

Prayer: Lord, I understand the truth of what you say. I can speak the right words, I can even do the right things, and yet my heart can remain far from you. In truth, I so rarely defer my will to yours. I choose to follow my own version of faith and faithful living, instead of just practicing what you preach. Lord, help me to go "all in" on your ways. Help me to trust that your way of living is better than my own. Encourage me to practice what you preach until I can fully appreciate the blessing of following your will for me. In your name, I pray. Amen.

Firm Foundation, Faithful Lord

"Everyone then who hears these words of mine and acts on them will be like a wise man who built his house on rock. The rain fell, the floods came, and the winds blew and beat on that house, but it did not fall, because it had been founded on rock. And everyone who hears these words of mine and does not act on them will be like a foolish man who built his house on sand. The rain fell, and the floods came, and the winds blew and beat against that house, and it fell—and great was its fall!" Now when Jesus had finished saying these things, the crowds were astounded at his teaching, for he taught them as one having authority, and not as their scribes.

MATTHEW 7:24-29

Reflection: Most Christian children and adults have a belief that Jesus was a carpenter. We have been told in church school and read in our Bibles that Jesus was, like his father Joseph, a carpenter. Art, books, and movies have all depicted our Lord as a worker of wood. However, one of the curious features of Jesus' teachings in the Bible is that he never uses carpentry metaphors, images, or illustrations to make his points. He uses agrarian images and hospitality illustrations, but hardly anything about wood and woodworking. A visit to the Holy Land reveals to the even mildly perceptive pilgrim that wood is scarce and the primary building material is stone. The

Greek word translated into carpenter is *tektōn*, which simply means builder. Likely, the English composers of the King James Version of the Bible were familiar with their own thickly forested landscape and assumed that Jesus would have built with the same materials the English used—wood. While Jesus rarely, if ever, used wood-working analogies to teach, Jesus continually referred to stone as illustrations for his teaching. It is more than likely that Jesus was a *mason*, and his sermons were informed by the stone with which he worked. Indeed, Jesus' final instruction in his Sermon on the Mount seems to proceed from a knowledgeable mason.

Jesus knew, like every good builder, that the foundation of a structure needed to sit on stone, not sand. To be secure, you should not ground your life on sifting and shifting matters and materials, but on the ultimate rock of our salvation: God and faith in God. By extension, grounding your life in the solid and sustaining teaching of Jesus was like sinking the footings of who you are right down to bedrock. According to Jesus, if you ground yourself in God and incorporate Jesus' teachings in your daily living, you will be stable, strong, and able to endure every storm that blows in your direction. God is the foundation, and as Jesus would say later in this same Gospel—Jesus is the cornerstone (Matthew 21:42). Jesus is the stone set in place that serves as a marker and guide for all the other stones in a building. Ground your life in God and align your life with the teachings of Jesus, and you will not be shaken, nor swept away by the currents that try to beat against you.

On a final note, Jesus as a stone mason, preaching with illustrations he understood from his vocational training, would have allowed him to communicate with great integrity. The concluding sentence of this section of Scripture affirms that Jesus spoke with a degree of authority and authenticity that was uncommon among the religious leaders of his day. Jesus' teaching, and the ways he expressed his instruction had integrity, weight, gravitas. Jesus spoke, and people wanted to listen and obey, because Jesus was trustworthy, wise, and dependable. We can trust Jesus. We can build our lives upon his words. Jesus is our firm foundation and our faithful Lord.

Firm Foundation, Faithful Lord

Question: What do you want your life to be built upon?

Practice: Reflecting on Jesus' sermon in its entirety, write out a set of foundational principles you want to live by and place them somewhere you can read them daily. In the months to come, strive to act upon them and maintain your practices.

Prayer: Lord, Master Builder, continue to craft my life in ways that are pleasing to you. Set me in place, make adjustments as needed, chip off my rough edges, and help me to be well-aligned with you. I want to be grounded in God and centered on you. Allow my life to rest on the Rock of my Salvation, and my living to be in line with the Cornerstone. In Jesus' name, I pray. Amen.

9 781666 763058